What Our Readers Have Said...

Applicability

"These books are great tools that should be used as guidelines for our everyday supervisory practices. You need to take the time to do a short self-evaluation when reading them."

•

"The things and problems we deal with everyday are discussed in these books."

•

Convenience

"I like this because I can take them with me to read at a convenient time. I feel the little time I have to spend in the office is best use on activities that directly relate to revenue opportunities. I like the short amount of time it takes to keep up with these."

•

"I just read each book, and then file it for future reference."

•

"I like the fact that the format allows the books to be reviewed as time permits. All work has been conducted on personal, evening/weekend time."

•

Challenge

"My thought is that the real value of these books comes into effect when doing the action plans."

•

"The challenge when I think a specific topic does not apply is to find a way to make it apply."

•

Clarity

"Short and sweet. These books are easy to comprehend."

•

"These books are very easy to read and clearly outlined."

•

"Easy to use, understand, and reference if needed."

•

Relevance

"I have enjoyed reading these books. They are relevant to today's work environment and the ongoing change in the way we manage our workforce."

•

"I believe the contents of the Pinpoint series are excellent. It causes one to reflect on the daily dynamics in working with oneself as well as with management and peers."

•

"I do feel that these books have been very helpful to me at my job."

•

"I do enjoy reading each of theses books and it gives some real thought to its instruction."

•

Managing Personal Stress & Burnout

Pinpoint Customer Service Skill Development Training Series

TIMOTHY F. BEDNARZ

MAJORIUM
BUSINESS PRESS

Pinpoint Customer Service Skill Development Training Series
"Managing Personal Stress & Burnout"
Timothy F. Bednarz

Graphic design: Monika Pawlak

Majorium Business Press
2025 Main Street
Stevens Point, WI 54481
715.342.1018 • 800.654.4935

ISBN 978-1-882181-57-5

Printed in the United States of America

Introduction

The Pinpoint Customer Service Skill Development Training Series is designed for targeted training and education regarding increased improvement in a specific skill or competency.

Each book within this series is designed to be easy to use, understand and apply to your job. It can be used as a basis for training individuals, as a discussion guide or as a personal training tool.

Each chapter within this book discusses a specific concept. When you have completed all eight chapters you should have a 360º perspective of the topic.

Additionally, each chapter is divided into specific sections:

- The first section provides you with an overview of the topic
- The Implications section discusses why the concept is important, and why it is important to learn and apply.
- The Strategies, Tips & Techniques to Apply section teaches how to use and apply the particular concept to your work.
- The Points to Ponder section gives you something to think about or to be discussed with a group setting. These are questions not meant to be immediately answered, but to be pondered over time.
- The Training Activity section provides you with the tools to transfer what you have learned to your job. It is designed to help create an action plan to effectively apply the concept.

Each of the topics in this series is time-tested and proven in the marketplace. They have been used by thousands of employees as training tools. Many of the users have commented that what made these books valuable, was the ability to refer to them when a problem surfaced. They indicated that they remembered reading about the exact problem. They referred back to these books and found an appropriate solution.

You will find them equally valuable as a resource in your professional development library.

Table of Contents

LEARNING OBJECTIVES:

- To understand the differences between stress and burnout.
- How to manage stress.
- To recognize burnout.
- To work through personal burnout.

1

Unmanaged Stress

Stress and burnout are real issues that most service representatives must contend with if they are to remain effective. Since these individuals are in the front lines as the liaison between the customer and their company, they are constantly dealing with anxiety, frustration, hostility and conflict. The very nature of their job is stressful and it is important for service representatives to learn to manage stress and avoid personal burnout.

IMPLICATIONS – WHAT THIS MEANS TO YOU

Many service representatives feel that stress is part of their job. If it gets to the point that they are unable to handle it, most will change jobs. However, this is not a permanent solution. It may reduce the levels of stress for a time, but the strain remains, as do the consequences of unmanaged stress on their lives and bodies.

Anxiety and tension are a large part of customer service representatives' jobs. The key for them to remember is not to try to avoid it altogether, but to handle it in a way that they are able to manage the negative effects.

STRATEGIES, TIPS & TECHNIQUES TO APPLY

Many people either ignore mounting pressure and strain or take specific actions to counter it. These actions may include using drugs or alcohol to minimize the stress or forget it altogether. While these behaviors are common, they are unhealthy because they fail to address the causes of the problem and only serve to mask the symptoms. Rather than solve the problems, these behaviors actually complicate the problems and further deepen the levels of stress. Individuals must recognize the consequences that the toll of unmanaged stress can take upon their lives. These include:

Addictive Behaviors

People who are under pressure will often not only increase the use of illegal drugs and alcohol, but may also increase the use of tobacco, prescription medications and other substances to help them cope. Individuals should be aware that these substances place them at greater risk for both physical and psychological dependence. It is important that individuals can become addicted to behaviors as well as substances. These can include fighting and hostility, overeating, verbal abuse, bullying, sexual excesses and other dependent and destructive behaviors.

Relationship Distress

While service representatives are not expected to be "chummy" with their customers, a sense of friendliness is appropriate. Some may feel comfortable displaying a level of detached concern toward their customers, which in moderation can be an appropriate behavior and even required for effective performance. However, when detached concern becomes excessive, it develops into depersonalization that can lead to callousness and cynicism with subsequent negative effects on the customer relationship.

Depersonalization—a behavior where individuals treat others like objects—is a mechanism many service representatives will use to minimize emotional involvement with their customers. These behaviors are observable in highly bureaucratic atmospheres and companies such as utilities and large phone companies, where service representatives are the constant targets of customer wrath.

Emotional/Behavioral Consequences

One of the most obvious manifestations of unmanaged stress in individuals is a change in their personal and emotional behavior. As they experience higher levels of stress, they can become more hostile and belligerent toward customers, associates and family. Left untreated, these behaviors can escalate into physical abuse and bullying behaviors. While difficult to predict how any individual will react to stress, other symptoms can include irritability, verbal abuse, cynicism, insomnia, lack of focus and concentration, low productivity and fatigue.

Ultimately, service representatives in high and unmanaged stress environments will experience emotional exhaustion caused by the excessive psychological and emotional demands of customers, associates and management. Leaving them drained and depleted of personal energy, these individuals experience low morale, reduced effectiveness, burnout and health problems.

Professional Consequences

Over prolonged periods of time, unmanaged levels of stress results in feelings of depression and a sense of professional ineffectiveness and diminished accomplishment. Over time, service representatives whose behavior escalates to this level begin to feel that their actions do not make a difference. Over time this adversely affects their relationships with their customers, the customer's satisfaction and, ultimately, the outcome of the relationship.

POINTS TO PONDER — SOMETHING TO THINK ABOUT

1. How do you feel you are coping with the levels of stress in your job?
2. How does unmanaged stress impact your life and your job?

TRAINING ACTIVITY – APPLICATION & ACTION PLAN

1. Evaluate the levels of stress that your are experiencing in your job, based upon the following criteria:
   - Addictive Behaviors
   - Relationship Distress
   - Emotional/Behavioral Consequences
   - Professional Consequences
2. Identify any of the negative factors that may be present in each category that are symptomatic of stress-related problems.
3. Determine how each of these factors is affecting your personal life and performance on the job.
4. Determine which factors you have control over and whether you might need professional help from your physician to help you cope with them.

2

The Path that Leads to Burnout

Many customer service representatives start their jobs with unrealistic expectations and impossible goals that set the stage for disappointment and letdown. When reality hits them, they start down the path to physical, emotional, and mental exhaustion and, ultimately, burnout.

IMPLICATIONS – WHAT THIS MEANS TO YOU

The road to burnout is paved with good intentions. While having high aspirations and being an idealistic, hardworking perfectionist is admirable, unrealistic job aspirations and expectations are doomed to frustration and failure. The burnout candidate's personality will keep him or her striving with single-minded intensity until he or she crashes.

The potential for burnout increases dramatically depending on the individual's personality, their job description, and the company they work for. Hard driving, idealistic and self-motivated achievers who think anything is possible if they just work hard enough are likely candidates for burnout. The same is true of individuals who are rigid perfectionists with unrealistically high standards and expectations. It should be noted that individuals in a job with little recognition and few rewards move from a possible to a probable burnout candidate.

STRATEGIES, TIPS & TECHNIQUES TO APPLY

Customer service representatives can often find themselves proceeding through the various stages of burnout without being aware that they are doing so. Burnout is not a sudden "out of the blue" occurrence; individuals go through a series of progressive stages, including:

Honeymoon

During the honeymoon phase, customer service representatives feel that their jobs are wonderful. They are excited, energetic and enthusiastic about everything they do. The opportunities and possibilities appear to be limitless, yet because they have formed an unusually optimistic outlook, the stage is set for deep disappointment and letdown.

Awakening

Once service representatives realize that their initial expectations were unrealistic, they are immediately deflated and unmotivated. Rather than examine themselves and their own expectations, they place the blame on the job. As disillusionment and disappointment grow, these individuals become confused and are unable to pinpoint what is happening to them.

The typical response to this situation is to work harder to overcome the disappointment. However, service representatives soon discover that working harder only leads to increased frustration and exhaustion without improving their personal situation. Consequently, their self-confidence suffers as they begin to question their competence and personal abilities.

Brownout

Brownouts begin as initial enthusiasm and energy is replaced by chronic fatigue and irritability. Behavioral patterns change. Eating and sleeping patterns are altered. Ultimately service representatives become indecisive, and their productivity diminishes as the quality of work deteriorates. Coworkers and superiors may comment on the deterioration of personal performance.

Unless interrupted, brownout slides into its later stages. Service representatives will become increasingly frustrated and angry and project the blame for their difficulties onto others. They become cynical, detached, and openly critical of their organization, superiors and coworkers. They are beset with depression, anxiety and physical illness. Drugs or alcohol are often a problem.

Burnout

Unless service representatives understand what is occurring and interrupt the process or someone intervenes, brownout steadily progresses into full-scale burnout. Despair is the dominant feature of this final stage. This may take several months, but in most cases it involves three to four years. Individuals experience an overwhelming sense of failure as well as a devastating loss of self-esteem and confidence. They become depressed and feel lonely and empty.

When individuals enter this last stage, life seems pointless. There is a paralyzing, "what's the use" pessimism about the future. Individuals are physically and mentally exhausted. Physical and mental breakdowns are likely. Suicide, stroke, or heart attack are not unusual as service representatives complete the final stage of what started with high hopes, energy and optimism.

Phoenix Phenomenon

With time, individuals can rise phoenix-like from the ashes of burnout. They need to first rest and relax. It is important not to take work home. Many people fear that the work won't get done and they feel guilty for being "lazy."

In coming back from burnout, service representatives need to be realistic about their job expectations, aspirations and goals. They must create balance in their life. This includes investing more of themselves in their family and other personal relationships, social activities and hobbies. The key for service representatives is to balance their activities so they don't have such an overpowering influence on their self-esteem and self-confidence.

POINTS TO PONDER — SOMETHING TO THINK ABOUT

1. Were you aware of how burnout is a slow progression?
2. Do you feel you maintain a healthy balance in your life?

TRAINING ACTIVITY — APPLICATION & ACTION PLAN

1. Carefully analyze the description of each stage identified in this lesson.
    - Honeymoon
    - Awakening
    - Brownout
    - Burnout
    - Phoenix Phenomenon
2. Determine if any of the symptoms apply to you. Rather than be embarrassed, it is important to be honest with yourself to avoid further escalation.
3. Identify the stage of burnout that you may be in.
4. If necessary, seek professional assistance to overcome these problems.

3

Causes of Stress in the Workplace

Everyone experiences stress in their daily work lives. Some of these stresses are healthy and keep employees alert, productive and driven. However, other types of stress can be destructive and limit personal motivation. These are often the types of situations that many individuals must deal with on a regular basis to maintain both their productivity and effectiveness.

IMPLICATIONS – WHAT THIS MEANS TO YOU

Many employees have seen economic upheavals such as downsizing, layoffs, mergers and bankruptcies that have cost hundreds of thousands of workers their jobs. Millions more have been shifted to unfamiliar tasks within their companies and wonder how much longer they will be employed. Adding to the pressures are new bosses, computer surveillance of production, fewer health and retirement benefits, and the feeling that one has to work longer and harder just to maintain their current economic status. Employees at every level are experiencing increased tension and uncertainty.

Not only are customer service representatives experiencing increasing levels of stress within their own companies, but their customers also are feeling similar levels of stress within their companies. Both customers and service representatives have shorter fuses and are easily triggered into emotional responses that rapidly escalate problems into more complex issues. All parties feel that situations are out of control, increasing their sense of helplessness.

STRATEGIES, TIPS & TECHNIQUES TO APPLY

The working environment is creating various levels of stress that all employees must learn to deal with. Some of these pressures are caused by the actions of management, but quite often much of the stress experienced is the result of radical changes in the business and economic climate caused by quickening pace of technological advances in every business sector. Stress can be caused by:

A Sense of Powerlessness

A feeling of powerlessness is a universal cause of job stress. When employees feel powerless, they are susceptible to feelings of helplessness and hopelessness. Consequently, employees feel they are unable to alter or avoid the situation because they feel nothing can be done to change it.

Customer service representatives are in one of the most highly-stressed occupations. This is due to the need to respond to others' demands and timetables, with little control over events. Many service representatives complain of unclear job descriptions, too much responsibility and too little authority.

Job Descriptions

Every employee should have a specific, written job description. When employees are able to negotiate their job description, this does more to dispel their sense of powerlessness. It is a contract that employees are instrumental in writing. They have the ability to object to specific issues and insist upon inclusions. If there is a compromise, it is because employees have agreed to it. With a clear job description, all expectations are spelled out including those of the employee and his or her superior.

A good job description is time limited. All parties should agree upon a specific date for a review and revision. If employers and employees can't agree on what a job description should include, it is advisable that employees look for another job, either inside or outside of the company. Even during difficult economic times, if stress levels are to be reduced, it is important that a job be a source of satisfaction and respect.

When Employees Are a 'Square Peg in a Round Hole'

There is an old adage that says, "Find a job you love and you'll never work another day in your life." Most people spend about 25% of their adult lives working. If individuals feel they are the proverbial square peg in a round hole, job stress will result, hurting their productivity and taking a serious toll on their mind and body.

Individuals remain in a job that doesn't fit them or that they don't particularly like for many reasons. One is the "golden handcuff," where salary, pension, benefits, and "perks" keep an individual tied to their job regardless of stress consequences.

Many people are in jobs they don't like or aren't good at. The quick answer to reducing their stress levels is to get a job they like or one that better matches their skills, abilities and interests. This is often easier said than done, as some individuals have no idea what kind of job they would like or what kind of job would be better suited to them.

Work Setting

There are times when the work setting creates physical stress because of noise, lack of privacy, poor lighting, poor ventilation, poor temperature control or inadequate sanitary facilities. Settings where there is organizational confusion or an overly authoritarian, lassiez-faire, or crisis-centered managerial style are all psychologically stressful.

POINTS TO PONDER — SOMETHING TO THINK ABOUT

1. What types of stress are acceptable to you and which ones are intolerable?
2. What determines if the causes of stress are intolerable?

TRAINING ACTIVITY – APPLICATION & ACTION PLAN

1. Do you understand the possible causes of stress in your life? Examine the following major causes of job-related stress:
    - A Sense of Powerlessness
    - Job Descriptions
    - When Employees are a Square Peg in a Round Hole
    - Work Setting
2. Identify the specific areas that you think are problematic.
3. Are there additional causes of stress not listed in this lesson?
4. Identify specific circumstances or problems that relate to each area.
5. Determine whether there are any ways for you to directly reduce the causes of stress.
6. If there are areas out of your control, discuss them with your supervisor.

4

Understanding Some of the Myths of Stress

Stress is a pervasive force that comes in so many levels and forms that it is easily misunderstood. Well-meaning friends, associates and superiors can offer any number of tips for dealing with stress; unfortunately many of them are ineffective and can even worsen the situation.

IMPLICATIONS — WHAT THIS MEANS TO YOU

Many customer service representatives are placed in quick-paced, high-stress situations. In an effort to assimilate them into these jobs, many representatives will be told myths to help them deal with the job-related stress. This does them a disservice, because when the myths aren't fulfilled, they feel it is directly related to their actions and activities. This in turn creates a sense of guilt that increases their personal stress. Rather than understand how stress impacts and affects their lives, these employees are made to feel that these events and circumstances are within their control, when in fact they are not.

Before service representatives can effectively manage the stress in their lives, they must understand both the cause and their reactions to stress. Once they are able to understand how these factors interact with each other, they are able to control and manage their stress levels.

STRATEGIES, TIPS & TECHNIQUES TO APPLY

There are several myths and misperceptions regarding stress that many individuals maintain, including:

Myth #1: Levels and Causes of Stress Are the Same for Everybody

Depending upon their personality, experience and a host of other factors, every individual reacts differently to stress. One individual may think the strain and pressure are crushing, while others may not even consider the same circumstances to be stressful at all. Additionally, an individual's response to the same circumstances can vary from instance to instance depending upon what else is occurring in their lives at any single moment in time. If individuals are experiencing high levels of anxiety from a number of other sources, they can easily overreact to a relatively small event. The response depends on the totality of what is happening at any single point in time.

Myth #2: Stress Is Always Destructive

The real issue regarding stress is more how to manage it than how destructive it can be. Properly managed, stress is a positive force that leads to people being productive and happy. Stress that is either mismanaged or ignored can be destructive to an individual's health and can even be fatal.

Healthy levels of stress keep people alert, motivated and productive. It is only when these levels go to extremes that they become harmful. High levels of stress are often associated with overwork and excessive demands made of employees, yet what many fail to understand is that low demands on employees can be equally stressful. This is especially true when these individuals are motivated, energetic and results-oriented: when they cannot perform up to their expected levels of performance, they become stressed.

Myth #3: Stress Is Everywhere, So Nothing Can Be Done About It

Individuals can plan their lives so that stress does not overwhelm them. Effective planning involves setting priorities and working on simple problems first, solving them, and then going on to more complex issues. When stress is mismanaged, it is difficult for individuals to prioritize tasks and activities and place the appropriate levels of importance on them. All problems seem to be equal, and stress seems to be present everywhere.

It should be noted that many individuals create their own levels of stress through the demands they place upon themselves. While these expectations are work related, they are unrelated to their specific job. In many situations individuals create unrealistic and impossible levels of performance for themselves that go beyond what is actually expected of them by their employer. These individuals become obsessed with their performance and driven by the need to achieve results. When they are unable to perform to these levels, they create high levels of stress to compensate for their lack of "acceptable performance." Rather than understand their personal motivation, they will relate the stress to their job and place the blame on the employer rather than themselves.

Myth #4: The Most Popular Stress-Reducing Techniques Are Best

Since stress is based upon a host of factors that affect each individual in different and varying ways, no universal stress-reduction program is the most effective. Before individuals can reduce their levels of stress they must understand triggering factors, how they personally react to them, and the interaction of their own personal motivational factors. Once they understand their behaviors and motivators, individuals can learn how to manage the stress factors that trigger responses in them.

Myth #5: No Symptoms, No Stress

The absence of symptoms does not equate to the absence of stress. As previously stated, healthy levels of stress are necessary for individuals to be happy, motivated and productive. However, many individuals have the tendency to internalize stress when these levels are initially encountered in their lives. They subconsciously allow these levels to rise until they begin to manifest themselves as external symptoms. When this happens, they will seek professional help to deal with the symptoms and begin to take medication that further masks the symptoms of stress.

Myth #6: Only Major Symptoms of Stress Require Attention

Minor symptoms of stress are early warnings that an individual's life is getting out of hand and that there is a need to do a better job of managing stress. This myth assumes that "minor" symptoms such as headaches or stomach acid may be safely ignored when in fact they are warnings that something must be done to cut off the consequences of stress. By the time more serious symptoms begin to surface, they can already have caused major health and behavioral problems that demand professional intervention. It is too late to effectively prevent or reduce unhealthy stress.

POINTS TO PONDER – SOMETHING TO THINK ABOUT

1. Do you see these myths regarding stress being perpetuated in your workplace?
2. What misconceptions have these myths created in your workplace?

TRAINING ACTIVITY – APPLICATION & ACTION PLAN

Listed below are the six common myths regarding stress:

- Levels and Causes of Stress Are Similar for Everybody
- Stress Is Always Destructive
- Stress Is Everywhere, So Nothing Can Be Done About It
- The Most Popular Stress-Reducing Techniques Are Best
- No Symptoms, No Stress
- Only Major Symptoms of Stress Require Attention

1. Identify the myths that you "bought into."
2. Determine the reasons that you accepted these myths as fact.
3. Identify the impact these myths have had on your life.
4. Determine what you can do to correct these myths and their impact on your life.

5

Telltale Signs of Burnout

When individuals begin to feel burned out, they start to experience slowdowns in their work, a lack of desire to increase their responsibilities and feelings of being trapped in inescapable, no-win situations. No individuals are immune from burnout; all are at risk, even when they are aware of its symptoms and possible consequences. Job burnout does not occur overnight, but begins with small warning signs and clues. It generally does not become obvious until individuals are far into the depths of it and begin to feel the full thrust of its negative effects.

IMPLICATIONS – WHAT THIS MEANS TO YOU

As stress and burnout are insidious in that both progress in small and often unnoticeable, incremental steps, it is important for individuals to be aware of the warning signs and monitor for them in their daily lives and work. Signals tend to surface as symptoms generally associated with or related to other problems, circumstances and issues. Unheeded, stress-related symptoms progress until individuals dread going to work. Ultimately, burnout spreads to all aspects of their personal lives: it is rare to find people that are burned out at work energized and enthusiastic at home. Before this happens, it is important to learn how to manage daily occurring stress.

The rising demands placed upon customer service representatives at work can create imbalance in their personal lives. This leads to internal conflict, increased stress and, if left unchecked, total burnout.

One of the keys of stress management is to create a balance between work, family and recreational activities. When people are able to strike a proper balance, they have adequate channels to handle stress factors and maintain their levels of internal harmony, where constant worrying interferences are minimized to the point where they can be dealt with effectively.

STRATEGIES, TIPS & TECHNIQUES TO APPLY

There are specific telltale signs that need to be recognized and addressed that signal approaching burnout. While other causes and consequences can be responsible for creating burnout, several deserve closer examination. These signs include:

Loss of Personal Motivation

People have differing sources and types of personal motivation. What motivates one person may not motivate another. Some individuals are driven by the ability to make money, others by their efforts to be of service.

As people experience increasing levels of sustained pressure and anxiety, their personal situations and circumstances tend to minimize and ultimately overwhelm their motivational factors. Their drive becomes greatly undermined and ultimately eliminated, resulting in a total loss of any internal inspiration and desire.

It is important for individuals to learn how to manage their lives and activities in order to maintain high levels of personal motivation. When they successfully do this, they can sustain their personal momentum. Some techniques to help accomplish this include:

- Working on projects they can become enthusiastic about
- Setting small and attainable goals that create a sense of accomplishment
- Rewarding themselves for the successful accomplishment of particular goals, objectives, tasks and assignments

Demoralizing Work Situations

Many individuals are placed into work situations that are highly stressful where they feel extremely helpless and generally "out of control." These can include ambiguous work assignments, having to deal with critical superiors, addressing hostile and angry customers, the lack of professional recognition or tangible rewards, and heightened workloads. These situations tend to create rising levels of personal anger and frustration.

Individuals need to know what is expected of them. They must be able to clarify and fully understand what their responsibilities are and the specific ramifications attached to them, including:

- The scope of their jobs
- The direction they are expected to take
- How their jobs fit into their respective organizations' goals and objectives
- Their organizations' specific goals and objectives

Information that applies to these issues is available within most organizations but often requires probing and research to uncover the answers. Once individuals become totally informed they are less likely to feel helpless and personally out of control.

Physical Breakdowns

The consequences of physical breakdowns are often seen and experienced only after individuals have allowed their stress levels to mount without adequately addressing them. Disorganized thinking patterns, head and backaches, occasional forgetfulness and overall fatigue often signal the emergence of possible physical breakdowns. When symptoms are left untreated, most individuals begin to become skeptical and judgmental, often vocalizing their negative emotions while displaying a lack of patience. Some begin to rely on drugs and alcohol to cope with their symptoms and situations. This can easily escalate into deeper and more serious problems.

Individuals must manage their personal lives. This includes:

- Getting plenty of rest

- Exercising daily and frequently
- Maintaining continual contact with friends and family

POINTS TO PONDER — SOMETHING TO THINK ABOUT

1. What factors in your life make you feel helpless?
2. Why do these factors make you feel this way?

TRAINING ACTIVITY — APPLICATION & ACTION PLAN

There are three keys to maintaining acceptable levels of stress in order to eliminate the possibility of burnout, including:

- Maintaining and Increasing Personal Motivation
- Managing Your Work Situation
- Maintaining Your Physical Health

1. Conduct a personal check within each category.
2. Identify specific areas that need to be addressed.
3. Take specific actions to eliminate or minimize the factors within the areas you identified.

6

Working Out of Burnout

Burnout is not a suddenly occurring condition, but a progressive wear-down ranging from normal feelings of getting somewhat tired of the job to a state of complete exhaustion. Most workers suffer from some of the symptoms of job stress, if not burnout, from time to time.

IMPLICATIONS — WHAT THIS MEANS TO YOU

The degree of personal burnout experienced by individuals will vary according to their tasks, assignments, responsibilities and their personal response to them. Some episodic burnout events can be attributed to high-pressure projects or problems that must be resolved or completed in a short time period and that elevate the intensity of circumstances. Since individuals may need to work at heightened levels of stress until these projects are completed or the problem is resolved, they are likely candidates for burnout. Burnout can become serious if individuals must work in an environment where they must deal with one problem or project after another without letup.

This is important for customer service representatives to understand because by both careful examination of the factors contributing to their stress and attending to their needs for well-being, they can usually halt the wear-down and revive their enthusiasm for their jobs. Individuals must conduct a frequent, in-depth examination of how they work and live in order to turn their stress into opportunities for personal growth.

STRATEGIES, TIPS & TECHNIQUES TO APPLY

Specific steps can be taken to overcome burnout. The problem is that many who reach this stage are not motivated to do anything about it. However, these techniques will work if individuals apply them.

Overcome Denial

When individuals are exposed to stress over long periods of time, they tend to deny that there is a problem. The first step is for individuals to learn to cope with their job stress. They can accomplish this by listening to the signs and signals of their bodies. They must freely admit and come to accept that they are under stress. They must identify the sources of their stress and learn how they are reacting to them. It is impossible to come to terms with burnout while individuals are still denying that there is a problem.

Avoid Isolation

When individuals are burdened with constant job stress, dealing with other people is often the last thing they want to do. This is despite the fact that developing closeness and emotional intimacy with others is one of the most effective ways for people to buffer themselves against pressure. Emotional intimacy creates new insights and decreases the negative effects of agitation and depression.

Reduce Personal Intensity

Individuals need to examine the areas of their lives that involve the most concentrated intensity. Once identified, individuals must work toward alleviating those pressures. This can involve both work and personal tasks.

Pace Time and Activities

People need to balance their time and activities. All individuals must learn to balance their work activities with their body's need to rest. This means individuals require both moderation and balance: they can work intensely for a while, but then need to take a break to reduce their loss of efficiency and productivity. It is important for individuals to schedule both quiet and relaxing interludes into their daily routine to keep themselves fresh and productive.

Minimize Worry

Many individuals tend to worry about the future. Often those worries never materialize. Worrying solves few problems, but does increase individual levels of general anxiety.

Maintain Physical Needs

When individuals allow their bodies to run down, they become more susceptible to burnout. They can balance and maintain their physical needs with a proper diet, adequate exercise, avoiding addictive substances and getting plenty of sleep.

Nurture Oneself More Than Others

Likely candidates for job burnout are those who are more concerned about the needs of others to the personal detriment of their own needs. Some people seek the approval of others by agreeing to take on enormous projects and working long hours. Individuals must learn that rather than nurturing others as their first response, they should try nurturing themselves. This often entails learning to say "no" as well as delegating responsibilities to others rather than taking on an overload.

Examine the Meaning of Work

Individuals must learn to identify what is meaningful in their life and separate it from those things that are temporary and fleeting. They must learn what is essential for their happiness. This includes examining how their work can become a reflection of their essential self. If this is impossible, then individuals should consider ways to modify their current job or perhaps go into a new career altogether.

POINTS TO PONDER — SOMETHING TO THINK ABOUT

1. Have you experienced periods of burnout in your life?
2. What techniques did you personally use to eliminate and overcome burnout?

TRAINING ACTIVITY — APPLICATION & ACTION PLAN

1. Examine the techniques that can be used to both manage your personal stress and eliminate burnout listed below:
    - Overcome Denial
    - Avoid Isolation
    - Reduce Personal Intensity
    - Pace Time and Activities
    - Minimize Worry
    - Maintain Physical Needs
    - Nurture Oneself More Than Others
    - Examining the Meaning of Work
2. Under each technique, identify how you can make it applicable and meaningful to you.
3. Determine how to apply each to your life.
4. Monitor these activities and their impact on your life.
5. Learn to make appropriate changes to increase your personal effectiveness.

7

Burnout: An Experience of Awakening

Burning out can be a terrifying experience. Many individuals tend to spend most of their waking hours on the job, oftentimes putting more hours into work-related activities than with their families and friends. When this enormous part of their lives becomes increasingly stressful, along with associated worry, self-esteem issues, anger, depression and withdrawal, a major personal crisis often results.

IMPLICATIONS — WHAT THIS MEANS TO YOU

When people experience burnout their initial impulse is often to deny the fact that job stress is finally getting the best of them. Most preserve the status quo and keep doing the same things every day, working even harder as though it might be the answer for finding relief. But the cycle is futile, as more work never alleviates the ill effects of working too hard but only further depletes one's emotional reserves.

When considering the concept of burnout itself not as something entirely negative, but more as an experience of awakening, service representatives will get an entirely new perspective. The personal events and symptoms leading up to burnout will help inform them that something is out of kilter in their lives, where they must look more deeply at themselves and how they function and react in order to find answers. Without a burnout crisis, many may never feel prompted to answer some critical and reflective questions about what is going on in their lives. Without this personal intervention, stress levels tend to increase and numerous burnout episodes result that tend to generate serious detrimental problems.

STRATEGIES, TIPS & TECHNIQUES TO APPLY

People faced with possible burnout are forced to deal with numerous issues stemming from the stress-related factors that ultimately lead up to it. To eliminate and minimize burnout, it is necessary to make critical life style changes to ensure long-term health and prosperity. Some of the issues that must be dealt with include:

Personal Goals

When people reach the point of a burnout crisis, they are forced to examine their personal goals and objectives. They must also determine if they are being honest with themselves. Many individuals enter into particular jobs or careers based upon others' expectations and aspirations, not their own, or because they look at their careers and positions as temporary and something to endure until "something better comes along." When individuals are not true to themselves, inner turmoil and conflict emerge that result in mental and physical stress and, ultimately, burnout. There are several fundamental questions that can be used to spotlight sources of turmoil and conflict in relationship to work, which are:

- What am I trying to accomplish with my work life?
- What are my key interests and does my work fit with them?
- What are my key skills and does my work use them?
- What are my core values with regard to life balance, family, money and the treatment of people? Is my work in harmony with these?

Individuals who find that their key interests are not aligned with the interests of the company they work for become mired in internal conflict. This includes any differences in core values or beliefs. If companies have low ethical values, then individuals with higher standards are required to do things that they personally oppose. They have to question the costs and losses associated with personally receiving their paychecks.

Additionally, if individuals have specialized skills, expertise and talents that are underused by their employers, stress results because of being held back. Rather than reaching their limits for growth potential, they become personally hampered. While many individuals may not outwardly feel this way, they nevertheless subconsciously experience elevated levels of stress.

Life Style Issues

When burnout occurs, individuals are forced to deal with specific life style issues that cause internal levels of heightened stress. Some questions that address these issues include:

- Am I overworking? If so, why?
- Where is the balance in my life between work and play?
- How would I live my life if I no longer had to work?
- What does work accomplish for me, and what is it preventing me from personally accomplishing?
- Can I shift the focus of my current work, or should I look into another type of job or profession?

Many individuals will forego specific life style changes in exchange for money, power and influence. In many other cases they end up in jobs where, due to the corporate culture, they are expected to put in long hours and are subjected to demanding bosses and superiors.

While some people thrive in these types of environments, others discover that when their lives are out of balance, they experience elevated levels of personal stress and, eventually, burnout.

Individuals must come to terms with the fact that different things motivate different people. When they examine their personal life styles and understand what is truly important to them, they are able to weigh, analyze and measure what motivates them and why. Once this is accomplished they can begin to adjust their lives accordingly.

Some people feel trapped in their circumstances yet refuse to adjust their lives in order to be true to themselves. They will continue to experience increased levels of stress and multiple episodes of burnout until they have no alternative but to change their lives.

POINTS TO PONDER — SOMETHING TO THINK ABOUT

1. What is your perspective when events like burnout occur in your life?
2. Do you feel victimized by your circumstances?

TRAINING ACTIVITY — APPLICATION & ACTION PLAN

1. Examine the following issues:

   Personal Goals

   - What am I trying to accomplish with my work life?
   - What are my key interests and does my work fit with them?
   - What are my key skills and does my work use them?
   - What are my core values about life balance, family, money, and the treatment of people? Is my work in harmony with these?

   Life Style Issues

   - Am I overworking? If so, why?
   - Where is the balance in my life between work and play?
   - How would I live my life if I no longer had to work?
   - What does work accomplish for me, and what is it preventing me from personally accomplishing?

- Can I shift the focus of my current work, or should I look into another type of profession or job?

1. Answer the questions listed above and determine how your answers affect your personal perspective.
2. Identify specific concerns and issues that have surfaced from your analysis.
3. Based upon your analysis, determine specific changes that you need to make.
4. Identify the choices and options available to you and make the appropriate decisions.

8

Reducing Regular Stress Levels

Many people make a serious mistake when it comes to dealing with their personal stress. They will often use alcohol, tobacco, illicit drugs and other substances and even shopping sprees to elevate their moods, while simultaneously continuing to increase their personal stress levels. This causes a rollercoaster effect of wildly swinging emotions that leave individuals feeling totally imbalanced and out of control.

IMPLICATIONS – WHAT THIS MEANS TO YOU

Many individuals have a tendency to self-manage and self-medicate in efforts to reduce and eliminate their personal stress. This often results in having their lives quickly spiral out of control due to a lack of internal balance. Rather than effectively improve their situations, individuals find that their stress levels continue to elevate. More importantly, as their stress increases, they feel that events are also rapidly increasing in pace and intensity. This in turn does not provide them with the time and opportunity to rest, which is needed for allowing their bodies to renew and regenerate.

It is important for customer service representatives to understand that reductions in personal stress levels can be achieved by eliminating the specific sources of it. Many of these sources can be easily controlled, while others may require some hard decisions. In either case, the choices and options cannot be ignored.

STRATEGIES, TIPS & TECHNIQUES TO APPLY

While some specific techniques to overcome personal burnout were detailed in previous lessons, there are certain ways that individuals can reduce their personal stress levels that ultimately tend to lead to burnout. These include:

Regulate Sleep Patterns

Sleeping difficulties are the hallmark of elevated stress problems. When internal body clocks stop working, individuals often have trouble falling and staying asleep. Some individuals may feel drowsy all the time. Either symptom may be experienced at intermittent intervals. It depends on the "position" their clocks are at when they stop: wakefulness or sleepiness.

When individuals suffer from elevated levels of personal stress, it signals that they have disrupted the function of their internal clock. Resetting it is essential for feeling energized, sleeping soundly and waking refreshed.

In order to reset one's internal clock it is imperative to establish set, definite wakeup and sleep times. This establishes a frame of reference. It generally takes two or three weeks to synchronize an individual's body clock to a regular schedule.

Allow Time to Heal

When individuals are experiencing elevated levels of stress, they need to allow their bodies adequate time to regenerate. Elevated levels of personal stress generally include the following symptoms:

- Fatigue
- Aches and pains
- Anxiety
- Problems sleeping
- Lack of enjoyment of life
- Depression

One effective technique individuals can use to reduce stress in their lives includes making a daily list of the things that must get done. Once it has been created, the bottom half of the list should be cut away and eliminated. Most of the tasks and responsibilities that fall into the lower half of the "things to do" are generally unimportant and will not be missed if left unattended.

Reduce Social Engagements and Commitments

In addition to associated work-related stresses, many individuals tend to increase their levels of stress with excessive social commitments. Hosting parties, events and dinners can greatly increase personal stress. Unless they are job related and required by superiors, individuals should reduce their personal commitments.

Postpone Changes in Living Environment

The biggest source of stress is directly related to "change." When individuals experience high levels of stress the last thing they need is to make changes in their personal lives and daily living environments. This can include moving into or remodeling a house or apartment. Even if certain changes are exciting, they still are a source of stress, and should be postponed until other events and circumstances have settled down.

Reduce the Number of Working Hours

Every additional hour that individuals spend at work over 40 hours increases levels of stress in their lives. While there are instances when additional time may be necessary and required, individuals should moderate their working hours to increase balance and harmony in their daily lives.

Keep Blood Sugar Levels Steady

Individuals who tend to experience elevated levels of personal stress almost always use sugar as a general "pick-me-up." What few realize is that when they do this, their blood sugar levels become destabilized. As blood levels continue to fluctuate they begin to experience wide mood swings, which have obvious effects on accompanying stress levels. It is important to pay attention to and maintain healthy blood sugar levels.

Avoid Allergies

Allergies are a major source of stress for many individuals. As the body must summon all of its resources to actively fight onslaughts of irritating agents, it can become run down. Left untreated over time, allergies will lead to individuals finding themselves drained of energy, exhausted, mentally depressed and physically ineffective. Individuals should not minimize the impact that allergies can have on their health and lives.

Exercise Regularly

The value of exercise three times a week for 20 minutes to two hours cannot be over emphasized. Enjoyable exercise in moderation elevates personal moods in a smoothly sustained fashion. It has the benefit of making individuals feel better in a relatively short period of time.

Exercise has another beneficial effect. When exercising, most individuals do not worry, but are instead actually resting the nerve cells in their brains generally used to fight anxiety and worry. Exercising allows time for these nerve cells to renew, regenerate and function normally until they are needed to help overcome another stressful situation.

POINTS TO PONDER – SOMETHING TO THINK ABOUT

1. How closely do you pay attention to the specific emotional, physical and social factors that impact your stress loads?
2. Did you realize that you can manage many of the stress levels directly affecting your life?

TRAINING ACTIVITY — APPLICATION & ACTION PLAN

1. Identify the sources of personal stress within each of the following categories:
   - Sleep Patterns
   - Healing Time
   - Social Engagements and Commitments
   - Changes in Living Environment
   - Working Hours
   - Blood Sugar Levels
   - Allergies
   - Exercise
2. Determine whether the specific stress triggers you have identified are within your control or not.
3. Determine how to manage the stress triggers within your control.
4. Identify the specific steps you need to take to reduce your stress load.

About the Author

Timothy F. Bednarz, Ph.D. is CEO of the American Management Development Group, Inc. For over 20 years he has researched, designed and authored hundreds of learning and development programs used by Fortune 1000 companies.

He is also the author of *Great! What Makes Leaders Great. What They Did, How They Did It and What You Can Learn from It* (2011).

Speaking Availability

Timothy F. Bednarz, Ph.D. is available for speaking engagements for your next meeting or association event. He can be contacted at 800-654-4935 or by e-mail at timothy.bednarz@majorium.com.

Bulk Sales

Bulk sales of this book or any other titles available from Majorium Business Press. Inquiries can be directed to sales@majorium.com, or by phone at 800-6654-4935.

Quick Order Form

Fax orders: 715-342-1118. Send this form.

Telephone orders: Call 800-654-4935 toll-free. Have your credit card ready.

Email orders: sales@majorium.com

Postal orders: Majorium Business Press, 2025 Main Street, Stevens Point, WI 54481, USA.

Please send the following books:

____

____

____

____

Please send more FREE information on:

❑Catalog ❑Speaking/Seminars ❑Mailing Lists ❑Consulting

Name: ________________________________

Address: ______________________________

City: ________________ State: ____ Zip: ______

Telephone: ____________________________

Email address: __________________________

Sales tax: Please add 5.5% for products shipped to Wisconsin addresses.

Shipping by air:

United States: $4.00 for first book and $2.00 for each additional product.

International: $9.00 for first book; $5.00 for each additional product (estimate).

Made in the USA
Monee, IL
08 November 2026

67380803R00031